P9-DVM-972

Pharrell Williams

Jennifer Strand

abdopublishing.com

Published by Abdo Zoom™, PO Box 398166, Minneapolis, Minnesota 55439. Copyright © 2017 by Abdo Consulting Group, Inc. International copyrights reserved in all countries. No part of this book may be reproduced in any form without written permission from the publisher. Abdo Zoom™ is a trademark and logo of Abdo Consulting Group, Inc.

Printed in the United States of America, North Mankato, Minnesota
102016
012017

Cover Photo: Dimitrios Kambouris/Getty Images
Interior Photos: Dimitrios Kambouris/Getty Images, 1; Anthony Mooney/Shutterstock Images, 5; Seth Poppel/ Yearbook Library, 6; Shutterstock Images, 7, 9, 19; Jeff Kravitz/FilmMagic, Inc/Getty Images, 8; Mark Allan/ AP Images, 10; Frank Micelotta/Invision/AP Images, 12; Michael Kovac/WireImage/Getty Images, 13; John Shearer/ Invision/AP Images, 14; Alex J. Berliner/ABImages/AP Images, 15; Richard Shotwell/Invision/AP Images, 17; Featureflash Photo Agency/Shutterstock Images, 18

Editor: Emily Temple
Series Designer: Madeline Berger
Art Direction: Dorothy Toth

Publisher's Cataloging-in-Publication Data
Names: Strand, Jennifer, author.
Title: Pharrell Williams / by Jennifer Strand.
Description: Minneapolis, MN : Abdo Zoom, 2017. | Series: Stars of music |
    Includes bibliographical references and index.
Identifiers: LCCN 2016948681 | ISBN 9781680799224 (lib. bdg.) |
    ISBN 9781624025082 (ebook) | 9781624025648 (Read-to-me ebook)
Subjects: LCSH: Williams, Pharrell, 1973- --Juvenile literature. | Rap musicians
    --United States--Biography--Juvenile literature. | Singers--United
    States--Biography--Juvenile literature.
Classification: DDC 782.42164092 [B]--dc23
LC record available at http://lccn.loc.gov/2016948681

Table of Contents

Introduction

Pharrell Williams is a famous musician. He is a singer and songwriter. He **produces** songs for many famous singers, too.

Pharrell was born on April 5, 1973.
He lived in Virginia.

He liked to skateboard.
He also loved music.

Rise to Fame

Williams started a group.
It was called the Neptunes.

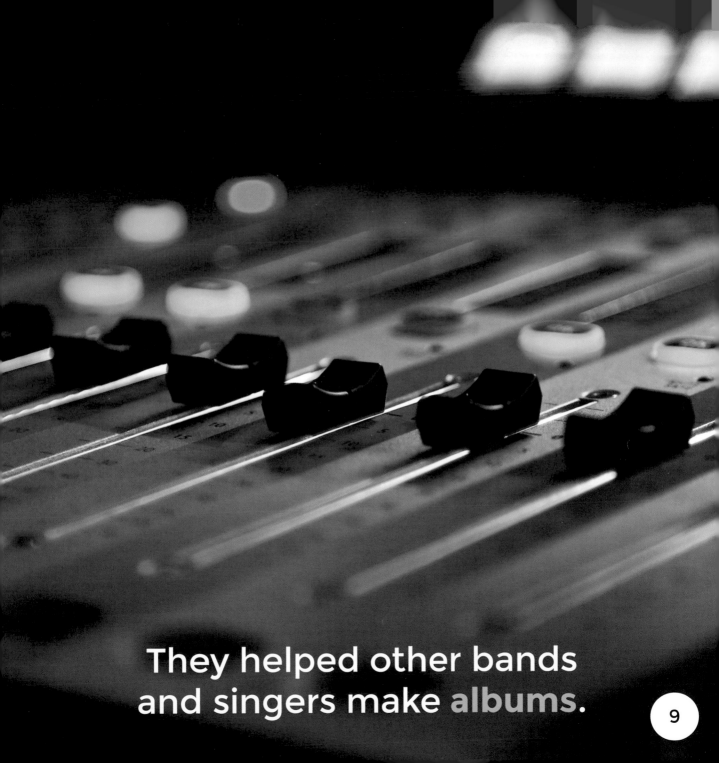

They helped other bands and singers make **albums**.

The Neptunes helped make many hit songs.

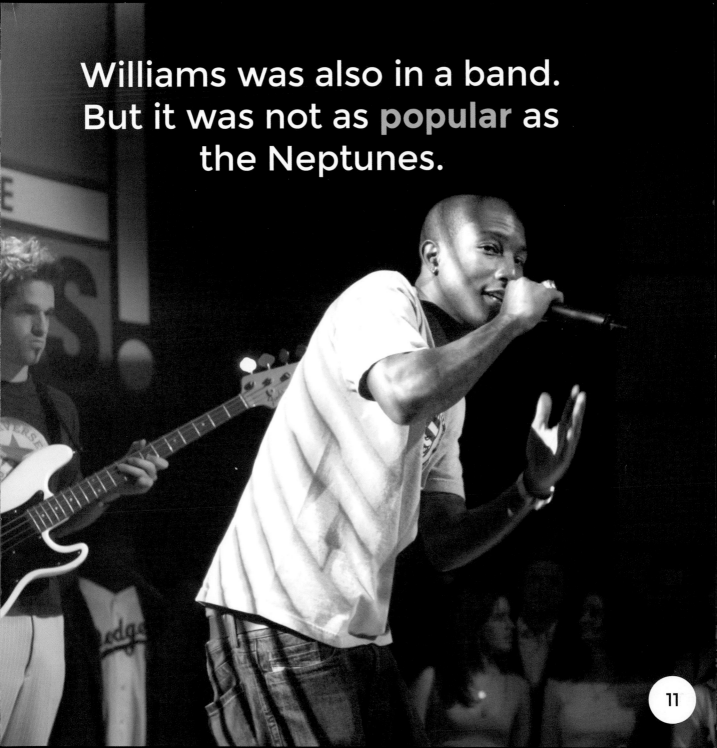

Williams was also in a band. But it was not as **popular** as the Neptunes.

Superstar

In 2013 Williams helped write two songs for other musicians.

They became big hits.

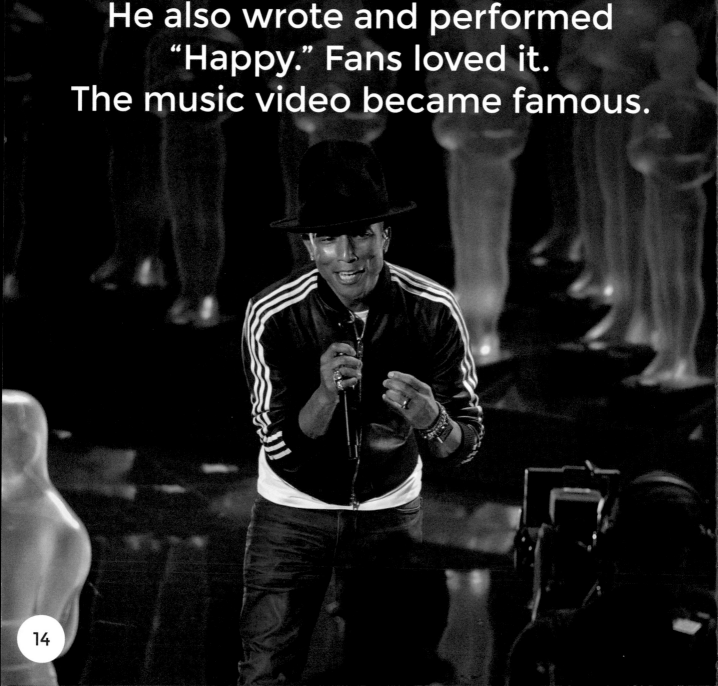

He also wrote and performed "Happy." Fans loved it. The music video became famous.

The song was featured
in a movie, too.

In 2014 Williams released a solo album. He also became a singing coach for *The Voice*. It is a reality TV show.

17

Now Williams is well known for his own music. He still produces music, too.

PHARRELL WILLIAMS

He has won many
awards for his work.

Pharrell Williams

Born: April 5, 1973

Birthplace: Virginia Beach, Virginia

Wife: Helen Lasichanh

Known For: Williams is a successful musician and producer. His hit song "Happy" went viral.

Key  Dates

1973: Pharrell Williams is born on April 5.

1992: Williams and Chad Hugo start a production team called the Neptunes.

2002: Williams's band N*E*R*D releases its first album.

2004: Williams starts his own clothing company.

2013: Williams's songs for Daft Punk and Robin Thicke become hits.

2014: "Happy" is the number one song in more than 90 countries.

Glossary

album - a collection of music.

popular - liked by many people.

produces - is in charge of and helps make a music album.

released - made available to the public.

solo - a performance by a single person.

Booklinks

For more information on **Pharrell Williams**, please visit booklinks.abdopublishing.com

Z**oom** In on Biographies!

Learn even more with the Abdo Zoom Biographies database. Check out **abdozoom.com** for more information.

Index